GLAMOUR

Copyright © 2009 Filipacchi Publishing, a division of Hachette Filipacchi Media U.S., Inc.

First published in 2009 in the
United States of America by
Filipacchi Publishing
1633 Broadway
New York, NY 10019

Design by Keith D'Mello

Metropolitan Home is a registered trademark of Hachette Filipacchi Media U.S., Inc.

Editor: Julie Gray
Production: Lynn Scaglione

ISBN-13: 978-1-933231-56-3

Library of Congress control number: 2008937590

Printed in China

Metropolitan Home

GLAMOUR
MAKING IT MODERN

BY MICHAEL LASSELL

Foreword by Donna Warner, Editor in Chief

Photographs produced by
Linda O'Keeffe, Creative Director,
and the editors of
Metropolitan Home

This book is dedicated to our mothers,
Catherine E. Lassell & Milburge D'Mello.

Not because they are particularly glamorous
(although they have both had their moments),
but because they taught us early that no place
is more beautiful than home.

—Michael Lassell & Keith D'Mello

*Contents

Foreword by
Donna Warner,
Editor in Chief of
Metropolitan Home   6

Introduction   8

CONCEPTS
Scale   16
Palette   24
Luster   34
Antiques   42
Asiana   50
Multiples   58

OBJECTS
Staircases   68
Fireplaces   76
Drapery   86
Chandeliers 100
Mirrors   110
Daybeds   118

ROOMS
Living Rooms   128
Dining Rooms   154
Kitchens   176
Bedrooms   196
Bathrooms   216

Resources   236
Credits   239
Acknowledgments   240

Glamour has never been one of my words. I do not consider either myself or my magazine, *Metropolitan Home*, especially glamorous—even though most of my family and friends would disagree. They imagine life in New York City as an editor in chief—traveling to amazing cities, seeing extraordinary homes, interviewing famous architects, going to press conferences and black-tie galas—a home design version of *The Devil Wears Prada*. However, when I asked my husband if he thought I was glamorous, he replied, "No, I think you're beautiful [smart man]. Glamour is fake, superficial." Since I've always prized depth and complexity, his point made sense. Add the snapshot of me writing this on a snowy January day: I'm sitting at my kitchen island, clad from head to toe in fleece (no Prada, just "Patagucci"), shivering from the winter morning's frigid barn work and frozen buckets. Glamorous? I don't think so!

In fact, I've always been somewhat suspicious of glamour. It conjures up 1930s and '40s film stars like Jean Harlow and Rita Hayworth, definitely beautiful and sexy, certainly provocative, but too glib and glossy for my more sensible tastes. I can't imagine them changing horses' blankets in a snowstorm.

So when we first began discussing the concept for this book, I wasn't especially enthusiastic. After all, our previous tomes had straightforward titles like *Renovate* and *Decorate*. *American Style* was a beautiful and clear compilation of *Met Home*'s modern world of design. All three featured photos of glorious homes, backed up by reams of helpful information. Both *Met Home* and I thrive on adding useful advice to beautiful moments—with mega doses of wit.

How would glamour fit into this habitual way of doing business? As I watched the group of editors getting more and more excited about the idea, I realized that a change of direction might be a good thing, right for the times, and refreshing, too. And then, as I read this book manuscript, I realized how totally wrong my original definition of glamour had been.

My about-face started with the way the photos are grouped. Instead of going through a house room by room and explaining how, where, when, and why, this book is a carefully constructed compendium of notions. Originally I thought this would be chaotic and confusing, but I was wrong again. (Did anyone ever define glamour as "eating your hat"?) I was wrong, too, that this organization would be superficial: Each Concept, Object, Room (the three sections of the book) and every individual photo contain a world of multilevel design lessons. What more could a pragmatic editor ask for?

As Bill Sofield says, "Real glamour is rooted in practicality." Little did he know how well that applies to this book. In fact, the designers' quotes are one my favorite elements of *Glamour*—they're all brilliant; each a small gem of insightful design wisdom that defines yet transcends glamour. How about "A room must have wit to be glamorous" (Jonathan Adler) or "When I think of glamour, I think of 'casual elegance,' natural ease, and simplicity, of having great style, making it seem effortless" (Carl D'Aquino).

So I've reconsidered: I now admire glamour, especially when it demystifies scale, palette, luster, multiples, the mix of Asiana, antiques and modern pieces. And who doesn't love drama-queen stairways, centerpiece fireplaces, elegant draperies, sexy chandeliers, Wicked Queen mirrors, soothing daybeds? Glamour, like elegance, is inherent and intrinsic. Instead of considering practical Polarfleece, I'm checking out my graceful horses as they play in the snow. In fact, it looks like a timeless movie, maybe *Christmas in Connecticut* (1945). I'll play Barbara Stanwyck's role.

Donna Warner, Editor in Chief
Metropolitan Home

What is glamour? Is it John Chrestia's pedigreed 1854 Greek-revival townhouse, one of many in New Orleans, or the architect's unique update, with the bedroom walls and fireplace painted the same color and furniture from the middle of the 20th century?

*Introduction

Of all the surprising developments in the world of home design of late, none was so unexpected as the reemergence of glamour as the dominant mode. Naturally, today's glamour is not identical to that of yesteryear, and—if you believe in the pendulum theory of progress—it might just be the logical response to pared-down minimalism, stark linearity, and the absence of decoration (just as all of those things were a reaction to the decorative excesses that preceded them). There is no doubt about it: Glamour has taken center stage.

But what is glamour? It's a lot like a color, really, say red: It's hard to describe without likening it to something else (like an apple, like a tomato), and there isn't just one kind (like a ruby, like a fire engine). And yet, most of us know it when we see it.

The first recorded use of the word dates from 1715, which means that neither linguist nonpareil William Shakespeare nor King James I, who commissioned the English translation of the Bible that bears his name, ever used the term, at least not in print. Surprisingly, "glamour" derives from a Scottish variant of the common English word "grammar." And its application relates to the presumed correlation between erudition and the occult. One could, at one time, speak of being "under a glamour," as being under a spell, or enraptured.

It is easy then to understand the relationship between glamour and such words as charm, enchantment, mystery, and magic. Further, "to glamorize" is a synonym of "to romanticize," particularly in the sense of the Romantic school of music, painting, and literature. Like that aesthetic movement, glamour incorporates the exotic, unusual, and esoteric. It is comfortable with exaggerated contrasts and unusual juxtapositions. It also embraces a sensuality that is erotic at its heart (even the luxurious fabrics associated with glamour get the libidinous responses flowing: velvet, satin, silk, and their soft-to-the-touch kissing cousins). There is no doubt that glamour isn't shy, either. It is, rather, extremely self-confident, which itself is sexy.

"When a client says 'glamour,'" says Los Angeles–based interiors and furniture designer Michael Berman, "it's code for 'Design our home so people will swoon when they visit.'" In other words, glamour has a palpable wow factor to it. "Glamour doesn't necessarily mean twinkly or sparkly," says designer and television personality Jonathan Adler: "There's rustic glamour, bohemian glamour, and butch glamour," to name just a few.

■ LARGE
Unlike most real-life rooms, this duplex loft—in a 1926 San Antonio candy factory that was converted by architects Jim Poteet and Patrick Ousey—is big enough to double as a soundstage for an elegant Fred and Ginger fox-trot. Deferring to the refined space, interior designer Courtney Walker exercised effective restraint.

■ SMALL
In the world of glamour, size doesn't matter. Matthew White made the most of the space in this 700-square-foot Manhattan two-bedroom by creating a neutral envelope made interesting by shots of cinnabar and pomegranate as well as custom and sculptural pieces, like a chair made of dominos by L.A. artist Clare Graham.

■ VERTICAL
Most designers agree that tall
rooms are the most glamorous.
Washington, D.C., architect Newell
Hugh Jacobsen designed this
Colorado home with soaring windows that exaggerate the ceiling
height, making the most of views
and incorporating nature into every
room. Who needs art with all that
natural beauty right outside?

■ HORIZONTAL
Tall rooms may seem to have more
obvious glamour potential, but
there's a low-slung alternative that
has its own allure. The ceilings of
this rambling Palm Springs home
designed by architect Donald
Wexler for singer Dinah Shore
in 1963 may not soar, but new
furnishings by designer D. Crosby
Ross are handsomely high style.

So what is glamour? That is the question *Glamour: Making It Modern* attempts to answer by example. The following pages include more than 200 photographs of rooms from some 125 different projects in the United States and abroad. The book is not so much an attempt to define glamour as to explore it. And to do that, the editors of *Metropolitan Home* reviewed thousands of photographs that have appeared in the magazine over the last five years and identified certain shared traits in rooms that were clearly glamorous—at least to us.

One of the first things that became obvious is that some of the most common assumptions about glamour are, in fact, misconceptions that should be put right. The first myth about glamour is that a glamorous room must be so large that the eye just cannot take it in. This is partly the fault of Hollywood, from which many of our 21st-century notions of glamour stem. The Dream Factory tends to create sets—from the streets of ancient Rome and the palaces of pharaohs, pashas, and British noblemen—that would dwarf the actual sites. Floor plans of movie rooms seem often to be measured in acres rather than square feet.

Now, enough room to breathe is highly desirable in any room, and several of the designers we spoke to for this book admitted that glamour suggested "lots and lots of space." But not everyone agreed. "Small rooms can be the most glamorous," suggests designer Matthew White of WhiteWebb in New York City. "Intimacy always has allure." And Chicago's Kara Mann asked (rhetorically), "Can a petite woman be glamorous?"

Furthermore, "space" can be literal or it can be a feeling about a room's not being full. Roominess can be implied by the negative space around objects as much as by the distance between walls. Glamorous modern rooms tend not to be crowded. "The least glamorous thing you can do in a room," says Washington, D.C–based designer Darryl Carter, "is fill the space just because it's there. I would rather have one great thing in a room than twenty space-fillers." There is great glamour in elegant restraint. Another myth, which is related, is that a room must be soaringly tall to be glamorous—a myth perpetuated in part by the double-height entryways of builder housing all over America. Open height (read: wasted space that's difficult to paint and impossible to furnish) can be glamorous, as architects discovered in the 12th century, when Gothic cathedrals started going up, and up, and up. But glamorous rooms can be gorgeously low-slung, too, especially in the idiom that has come to be known as midcentury modernism. Width can be as impressive as height.

What does seem true is that glamour likes exaggeration, either of height or width, and that more important than the aspect ratio of ceiling to walls is an aesthetically satisfying sense of proportion, so that the room itself, even when empty, seems perfect, a feeling the furnishings attempt to deepen and enrich rather than contradict.

The third myth is that glamour is necessarily expensive. Naturally, it often is: A Ferrari is, by definition, more glamorous than a Camry. Designers, however, are confident that glamour is more about a point of view than a client's access to disposable income. "Glamour doesn't have to break the bank," says designer Vicente Wolf, "but it should break the mold."

And what is a glamorous attitude? "When I think of glamour, I think of 'casual elegance,'" says Carl D'Aquino of D'Aquino Monaco, "a natural ease and simplicity of having great style and making it seem effortless."

Glamour: Making it Modern is divided into three sections. The first, called "Concepts," deals with some of the general notions that are associated with contemporary glamour. The subchapters—Scale, Palette, Luster, Antiques, Asiana, and Multiples—take a look at the ways these ideas work to bring glamour into our rooms. The second, "Objects," focuses on tangibles that you will find in many glamorous environments: Staircases, Fireplaces, Drapery, Chandeliers, Mirrors, Daybeds. The last section is titled, directly enough, "Rooms," and it is divided into Living Rooms, Dining Rooms, Kitchens, Bedrooms, and Bathrooms. Here we see how the various concepts and objects, passed through the prism of the designerly imagination, come together to create glamour. And while we think all of these rooms epitomoze glamour, many of the same decisions, or the same kinds of decisions, are involved in building or remodeling any room.

"The wonderful thing about glamour," says Michael Berman, "is that it is actually an obtainable concept. It is pairing the ordinary and extraordinary that creates the enchantment and illusion of unlimited funds. Humble products such as limed oak, grass cloth, sisal, cotton, and cork can be used as backgrounds with lacquer, silver tea paper, leather, and steel. These precious and simple materials, when married together, create a beautiful study in obtainable glamour on a budget."

But the bottom line in any room, intentionally glamorous or not, is personality, personality, personality. "No room (or home) is glamorous without love," says Nestor Santa-Cruz of Gensler in Washington, D.C. "The personality of the home should be that of the owners, not that of their architect or decorator."

Glamour may not appeal to all people, but it clearly appeals to many. And this book is dedicated to those who love glamour or find in it some inspiration for living in comfort, especially those who have embraced glamorous style, or who are about to by building a new home or renovating an existing residence. The book is full of ideas, so please feel free to use them. Enjoy the book, enjoy the glamour!

Michael Lassell
New York City, 2009

■ HIGH
For his Los Angeles home, designer Mark Schomisch assembled choice furniture, art, and accessories that quietly but unapologetically assert themselves as cultured, courtly, and genteel, from the gold-leaf–inspired wall covering above the fireplace to the sculptures that flank it. This room is chic, polished, and comfortably couture.

■ LOW
Young Miami designer Rita Motta did not have an unlimited budget when she designed her home, but she managed to create a uniquely glamorous ambiance with wit and ingenuity (she designed both the pillow and the red acrylic chandelier) and by shopping in second-hand stores and well-priced venues like West Elm.

*CONCEPTS

*Scale

At his home in Washington, D.C., Thai-born graphic designer Supon Phornirunlit created a white envelope for his living room and focused the conversation area on a colorful, overscale coffee table that doubles as an ottoman. The enormous shade on the floor lamp is made from scraps of faux fur.

■ Manhattan-based designer Vicente Wolf is known for chic, tailored, serene interiors peppered with Asian antiques—and for his love of mirrors. In this apartment in Stockholm, he created a dramatic entry by backing an 18th-century Chinese table with a huge leaning mirror that provides reflected light and an expanded sense of space.

■ San Francisco architect Abigail Turin wanted the eye to pass through "stages of lightness" from the living room of her family home to the adjacent terrace. She chose bulbous B&B Italia lounge chairs to match the walls and floor and amped up the contrast with a sculptural white-cotton floor lamp by Marcel Wanders for Cappellini.

■ The gallery-scale photograph of horses by Roberto Dutesco on the wall of building contractor Jim Dow's renovated lower-level family room in Seattle creates a sense of grandeur while it establishes a masculinity common to all the rooms and reflects the home's earth-toned color palette (interior design by Garret Cord Werner).

■ Nothing says luxury like over-scale furniture in smallish rooms. In the master suite of this house in the Hamptons, designers Sean Webb and Brent Leonard of Form Architecture + Interiors created a wall-to-wall upholstered head-board and added a full-figured white *Gaivota* chair by Brazilian designer Ricardo Fasanello.

"The most glamorous thing you can do in a room is to be surprising."—Jill VanTosh

Bigger is not always better. A Fabergé egg is only a few inches high, but you won't find an object with a more refined pedigree. Exaggerations in scale, however, and subtle manipulations of proportion—the relationship between the sizes of things—can produce the drama that we associate with glamour. There is little doubt that Michelangelo's *David* is immortal partly because it towers above us and the hand that threw the giant-killing stone is more massive relative to its arm than it would be in life. In the world of interior design, it is often more desirable to create a room from fewer, larger pieces than to fill it up with bits and pieces. Upping the scale of the objects—painting with large brushstrokes, as it were—tends to make rooms seem grander than their proportions, no matter how large they are. Playing oversize objects against normal or even undersize pieces can make spaces seem taller or wider, more or less open. Big pieces command attention the way a real movie star does on a red carpet crowded with lesser celebrities. "Grand" objects can create focal points, organize a room, draw focus, state or recapitulate design motifs, create architectural gravitas, and imbue a room with a gratifying sense of abundance and largesse. They are often also a great deal of fun.

■ Exploring the attraction of opposites in the living room of this Shigeru Ban house on Long Island, designer Shamir Shah contrasted massive natural shapes in the anchoring root coffee table and cast-metal side table with the delicate pieces of a wall-mounted sculpture from Paul Villinski's "Beer-can Butterflies" series.

"Oppositions by their very nature are extreme and therefore inherently glamorous."—Scott Joyce

"Part of being glamorous is taking risks." —Jay Jeffers

■ The owner of this home on Queen Anne's Hill in Seattle was so enamored of an antique Italian mirror that she bought it even though it was too tall to hang. So she leaned it on the floor, where it now echoes the doors and windows to its right, creating a grand virtual frame for social events.

■ For this well-edited Kansas City, Missouri, dining room, designer Kathy Kelly of Helix Architecture + Design chose a refined French table from the 1930s and found unity in the curves of a voluptuous Darcy Badiali sculpture, a graphic Richard Serra artwork, and contemporary chairs by Kerry Joyce.

■ In her own London dining room, British designer Kelly Hoppen went big with a horizontal India Mahdavi mirror that runs along the banquet-scale table and two leading lights: a custom pendant fixture (with deep fringe) by the wittily subversive Mat & Jewski of Paris, and an iconic *Anglepoise* floor lamp.

*Palette

■ New York CIty-based designer Benjamin Noriega-Ortiz attributes his joy in color to his Puerto Rican upbringing. Knowing that red stimulates the appetites, he saturated this monochromatic dining room north of New York City with a deep and vibrant version of the color; the adjacent living room is bathed in a warm honey mustard.

■ This horse-loving Long Island guest room by Form Architecture + Design celebrates the pure contrast of black and white. Here, white walls and snowy bed linens show off a black *Egg* chair by Arne Jacobsen that picks up the graceful curves in a Tim Steele pastel of a lasso over the bed and a vintage Blenko lamp base beside it.

■ In the upstairs sitting room of his Greenwich Village townhouse, which was renovated by Gisue Hariri and Mojgan Hariri, designer Michael Aram went for black and near-black accents in a white and near-white room trimmed in tones of one of white's most flattering costars: metallic silver.

■ A pair of empty nesters worked with designer Daren Joy to create this ethereally futuristic white-on-white home in Marin County, California. In the entire house the only color comes from pale wooden floors and the variations caused by shifting light. Like many designers, Joy chose Benjamin Moore's *Super White* for the walls.

■ If you think that a black space is not quite as glamorous as a white one, remember that Shah Jahan laid the foundation for a second, black, Taj Mahal directly across the Yamuna River from the white one he built. This mostly black kitchen was created by Kelly Hoppen for a single, male client in London.

"Red is always glamorous, but any color can be great if done with pizzazz!"—Vicente Wolf

Many of our ideas of glamour date back to films from the early decades of the 20th century and are, therefore, associated with black-and-white cinematography. Even today, white is the design world's favorite color. Some 60 percent of Benjamin Moore's paint sales are earned by its many shades of white. But the power of color is not to be discounted. When she was married to MGM chief Irving Thalberg, movie star Norma Shearer threw a studio ball with a strict black-and-white dress code, then made her own entrance at the top of a grand staircase dressed from head to toe in red. The Academy of Motion Picture Arts and Sciences created an Oscar category for best *color* art direction in 1940 (the first award was for Vincent Korda's Technicolor work on the richly jewel-toned *Thief of Bagdad*). What color is a glamorous room? The answer: It doesn't matter. It isn't the color but the manipulation of palette that packs the glamour punch. As the examples on the following pages show, a room can be black, white, black-and-white, neutral, monochromatic, or a color-wheel explosion. The color itself does not make a room glamorous: it is the often elaborate, yet con-trolled, way the color is applied by the room's designer that does so.

■ Black-and-white schemes are effectively given a shot of modernist energy with a bold accent color. Almost any color will do the trick, but none is more versatile than red. Betsy Burnham created this Beverly Hills bedroom with a four-poster of her own design and a bright-red chair by Hermann Czech from the Conran Shop.

■ For a house in Atlanta that is almost all white or neutral, designer Jill VanTosh went stark raving mod in the guest room, opting for flocked wallpaper, white furniture, and a watermelon-toned ceiling that picks up the color of the art. The hot, fruity hue works like the red sole of a black Christian Louboutin pump.

■ A traditional Craftsman bungalow in Atlanta got a bohemian-chic makeover for a photographer by designer Wendy Blount. Original architectural features meet Blount's modern sensibility in the dining room, where red accents include the art over the fireplace and a spectacular Murano-glass chandelier.

FARE THEE WELL,
LET YOUR LIFE PROCEED BY ITS' OWN D

LET IT BE

LET THERE BE SPACES IN YOUR TOGETHERNESS, AND
LET THE WINDS OF THE HEAVENS DANCE BETWEEN YOU

EVER HAS IT BEEN
THAT LOVE KNOWS NOT ITS OWN DEPTH
UNTIL THE HOUR OF SEPARATION

BE PRESENT

■ Chiaroscuro painters discovered that the high contrast of light and dark is provocative, evocative, and visually arresting. Chicago designer Kara Mann created a romantic, high-contrast entry to her own Goth-inspired loft with "bittersweet chocolate" walls, a vintage, antler-trimmed pine table, a photograph by Sally Mann, and a theatrically focused art light.

■ If there is drama in contrast, there is an inherent elegance in the tonal and textural subtleties of a monochromatic room. In this New York City master bedroom, designer Francine Gardner, who admits she is "not a color person," selected a massive oak headboard and sensuous, soft fabrics in warm and buttery shades of beige.

"Softly hued rooms are the most elegant and glamorous. I think the subtle tones of white, taupe, and my new favorite—burnt sugar—create the most soothing enveloping backgrounds."
—Michael Berman

■ No single color has a monopoly on glamour. In this Los Angeles home, designer Susan Moses transformed a shrinking violet of a kitchen by painting the cabinetry an au courant shade of chartreuse. She added textured glass door panels and installed CaesarStone countertops and backsplashes made of stainless steel mini tiles.

■ Some colors are riskier than others, but they're worth it (and all the extra coats usually required). This fashion-forward near-red *Fired Orange* shade from California Paints is striking in a Woodstock, New York, farmhouse updated by designer April Sheldon. Both the "hatbox" table and Cherner chair are midcentury pieces.

■ For a client's apartment in the Chelsea area of Manhattan, glamour-friendly designer Jamie Drake used different, but equally vibrant, color strategies in each room. In the dining room/office he lacquered the millwork with high-gloss blue and served up a jolt of citrus in the lime chenille fabric covering Troscan's *Ennis* chairs.

■ If any color can be glamorous, then all colors together must be even more glamorous. Or at least that appears to be the reasoning employed by designer/TV host Todd Oldham—who seems to love all colors equally and often—when he created this unique wall treatment for the kitchen of his own home in rural Pennsylvania.

Victoria Meyers and Thomas Hanrahan of hanrahanMeyers Architects in New York City let this warmly minimal apartment overlooking Central Park bask in the inner glow of stainless steel. Sleek closet doors and bookshelves of the same material contrast with a thick slab of ash wood fashioned into a polished counter by Japanese artisan Hisao Hanafusa.

*Luster

"Surfaces that reflect light and sparkle at the same time define glamour. Midas had the right touch."—Jamie Drake

All that glitters is not gold, and, in fact, gold does not so much glitter as radiate an enigmatic inner source of energy. Just as precious metals (gold, platinum, silver) make great jewelry, they make great room accents, as do a variety of their less-precious metallic neighbors on the chart of elements, like aluminum and copper, as well as alloys like brass, bronze, and even stainless steel (especially in modern settings). Lamps, side tables, vases, and collectibles of these and similar materials have been legitimately called the jewelry of glamorous rooms. Glamour revels in shine and sheen, whether natural or man-made, and rooms with glamorous agendas may well favor enamel finishes on floors, walls, and ceilings as well as on accessories. Modern interiors find the inner glow of glass and a variety of elegant synthetics—acrylics, Lucite, various polymers—to be likewise appealing. In keeping with the big mix of contemporary interiors, a glamorous interior is likely to mix and match a wide variety of subtly and overtly gleaming, glistening, and glinting surfaces. Fabrics, too, play their part, especially those with high silk or metallic content. Think of a sinuous chair that takes its inspiration from the bias-cut white satin dresses immortalized by Jean Harlow.

■ The allure of marble has captured the aesthetic imagination since antiquity. For his own Hollywood Hills kitchen, designer Mark Schomisch chose a dark variety called noir St. Laurent with a polished finish, which he had cut into "tiles" for the walls (because it scratches relatively easily, it is not recommended for use on floors).

■ The seductive sheen of gold also attracted Mark Schomisch, who wrapped the chimney breast in his Los Angeles bedroom with a Phillip Jeffries wall covering that mimics gold leaf. Gold, while precious, does not always need to be deadly serious; Schomisch used it as the background for a humorous painting of a duck by Todd Murphy.

■ In the bathroom of their master suite in Portland, Oregon, husband-and-wife architects Claudine and Giorgio Lostao installed a stainless steel countertop with an integral sink and brought the mirror right down to the horizontal vanity surface, extending the effect of infinite reflection; accessories include gleaming antique glass beakers.

■ When Julie Snow Architects designed this home in Minneapolis, the designers chose a pair of modern *Arctic Pear* chandeliers from Ochre for the large glass-enclosed dining room. The solid drops reflect the homeowner's centerpiece, made from her collection of mercury glass (a technique that dates from around 1840).

■ For this refined loft in New York City, designer Valerie Pasquiou happily inherited her client's Paul Evans table of mirrored chrome "tiles" from the '70s (the '70s loved patchwork). She chose Lucite chairs by Flou to create a dining room dazzling with reflection and transparency that augments the glitter but doesn't intrude.

■ Even the humblest of materials can be made glamorous if it has been shined up. For this octagonal dining room in Tucson, Arizona, architect Arthur Andersson specified a highly polished poured-concrete floor, which he scored to echo the ceiling coffers. Taking a lesson from Frank Lloyd Wright, he designed the dining table, too.

■ When innovative textile designer Lori Weitzner moved from her cozy cottage to a modern urban apartment in New York City, she married traditional and contemporary elements. Here, the timeless appeal of polished wood in the dining table (a door from the Philippines) meets B&B Italia chairs in one of her own typically silk-rich fabrics.

In his Chicago apartment, design dealer Andrew Hollingsworth raised the ceiling of his ample foyer to Byzantine heights with gold leaf in a classic application. To increase the light bounce in the windowless space, he installed a marble floor (the rest of the rooms have wood parquet underfoot), then hung two gold sconces like a pair of earrings.

When L.A. designer Darryl Wilson updated this 1960s cliff-hanger atop Hollywood Boulevard, he had the good sense not to disturb the original concave fireplace surround of bronze-toned ceramic tile. He did improve the seating in the conversation pit, the kind of place you might expect to find full of Rat Packers with their suave on.

"My favorite materials are burnished anything: Gold, silver, bronze ... the sunlight hitting any of these surfaces creates warmth." —Michael Berman

"Materials like glass, mirror, and Lucite can create the illusion of an expansive space, but too much will look like an art deco movie set." —Kelly Monnahan

*Antiques

When San Francisco designer Jiun Ho modernized a classic 1927 Nob Hill apartment for a European client, he hung the owner's set of lithographs by artist Antoni Tàpies and tied them both texturally and tonally to a Ming vase and the German 18th-century oak table the client used for a desk as a boy.

■ When assembling this home office in Beverly Hills, designer Betsy Burnham started with an antique Dutch desk, a crystal chandelier, and a traditional wing chair. The room's modern identity lies both in the palette and in the overscale prints in the rug and the drapery fabric, which bring inherited patterns into the 21st century.

■ It's her sophisticated design eye that enables Marjorie Skouras to incorporate antique and new pieces without creating visual chaos. In her Hollywood dining room, she marries of-the-moment metal chairs by Philippe Starck in a gold finish to handmade antiques and a chandelier of her own design with a coral-branch motif.

■ Chicago architect Charles von Weise retained the historic façade of his 1880s home, but blew out the back in a brightening modern renovation. The dining room, located beside a stunning von Weise staircase where the original house meets the addition, is furnished with French and English antiques that speak of history.

■ A major antique can make a room. In his bedroom, David Cruz—one of the partners in the cutting-edge Blackman Cruz showroom in Los Angeles—gave pride of place to a rare chair by Carlo Bugati (of the automotive family). To keep it in focus, Cruz placed it against a plain background on a "rag" rug made of leather scraps.

"Nothing looks less modern than a one-period room."
—Larry R. Laslo

Once upon a time in the world of modern interior design, anything old was considered patently non grata. Only the new was welcome to inhabit the most modern homes. But modern design is now more than a century old and no longer quite so insecure or suspicious of great design from days of yore. In fact, modern home designers have come to understand that there is a certain visual as well as emotional richness in using antique and vintage pieces side by side with the latest work from Milan. "We love to pair antiques in modern settings," says D'Aquino Monaco principal Carl D'Aquino. "I believe it is extremely hard to accomplish a dialogue between multiple periods, but when it is properly achieved, you are left with a truly glamorous and intriguing space." Some designers have gone so far as to suggest that anything that is well designed will "go with" any other well-designed object, no matter what the period or provenance. What makes a room modern is not so much what is in it but the relationship of the function of the room to its form. The marriage of old and new is, in fact, one of the hallmarks of the best-designed homes of the early 21st century. This mix in contemporary settings helps rooms transcend trendiness to achieve lasting and authentic style.

The master bedroom of a Seattle home renovated by prizewinning architect Tom Kundig features a rigorously modern steel and walnut custom bed designed by one of the homeowners. Its glamour is heightened by that of a deeply carved Spanish Revival table that echoes the geometry of the room while softening the severity.

For a contemporary renovation of a traditional upstate New York home, interior designer April Sheldon kept a 1920s foyer mural and added an anonymous unrefinished flea-market mirror and a refined Korean *tansu* chest to keep the mix thoroughly modern. The bright-red color for the living room walls was taken from the mural.

Nothing is more modern than the big mix. In his white-on-white apartment in Minneapolis, designer Andrew Flesher assembled his of-the-moment home office with an 18th-century French writing desk, a 20th-century "bank portrait," 1950s crystal sconces, and a recent Christian Liaigre leather chair from Holly Hunt.

Most of the furnishings in the living room of this converted 1896 Seattle school are appropriate to architect Eric Cobb's loft-inspired renovation, which includes a wall of dramatically pivoting windows. The single "antique," a French armchair upholstered in a high-gloss blue fabric, ties the room to history and gives it a welcome bit of sass.

"When a client says 'glamorous,' I think of the perfect blend of beautiful antiques paired with newer, more modern furniture."
—Carl D'Aquino

*Asiana

"A glamorous space makes you dream of other spaces."
—*Nestor Santa-Cruz*

Like the world economy, interior design has become more global, with influences coming from South America, Africa, and, especially, the Far East. Contemporary rooms can have the look of steamer trunks decorated with the stickers of foreign ports of call. The particular appeal of China and Japan are unique to modernism for several reasons. The "exoticism" of the East has been part of the European imagination since Marco Polo, and the golden age of film maintained the tradition with stars like Anna May Wong and films like *Shanghai Express* (nothing is more glamorous than a cinematically lit black-and-white shot of Marlene Dietrich beside an eight-foot art-deco foo dog). But the connections go much deeper. The great Impressionist painters of France embraced Japanese woodblocks, and the harmonious geometry of Asian architecture was adopted by early modernist builders in Europe and North America, Frank Lloyd Wright notably among them. As we grow in our concerns for the environment, we come to appreciate the unique relationship Asian decorative arts have always had with nature, and the serenity of Eastern philosophies and religions, especially Zen Buddhism, becomes more and more appealing as life gets more challenging.

■ Architect Lavinia Fici Pasquina wrapped an energy-efficient addition around her small 1940s house in Bethesda, Maryland, using insulated Nanogel panels for the new walls. In the loftlike modern living room, the panels are configured in a pattern that evokes Japanese rice-paper screens. Concrete floors have embedded radiant heating.

■ This indoor/outdoor dining room in a home designed by April Sheldon for a family of mixed Chinese and English ancestry is actually in Woodstock, New York. The electrified Chinese candle lanterns, the rustic table and chairs (or are they benches?), and the red accents make the room seem like an Asian country inn.

■ The master bath of this Boston apartment—built by Office dA architects, with interior design by Pappas Miron of New York—has Japan written all over it, from the river-stone shower floor to the window shutters and stool made of water-resistant teak. The moss-green tiles add to the natural appeal of the materials palette.

"The simple forms, clean lines, and restrained ornamentation of Asian design have always inspired anyone with eyes to see." —Matthew White

"Mixing different periods and countries of origin shows that you are a collector. It's a kind of bohemian way of thinking, an irreverence that is also elegant." —Carl D'Aquino

■ The residents of this classic art-deco duplex in Chicago hung some 1,000 of their prized photographs, many in the main stairwell and foyer. While there is a lot to see here, there is a method in the seeming mayhem; the simply and similarly framed images are grouped by theme and content.

*Multiples

"Any repeating geometric shape is glamorous." —Scott Joyce

I f you've ever sat in a Paris park and taken in the endless rows of chestnut trees as they follow invisible lines of perspective to the horizon, you know just how pleasing repetition can be. The same is true of decor. Almost any room will contain collectibles, curios, and souvenirs that define the people who live in it. Great designers have discovered that it is the way objects are displayed, as much as the objects themselves, that makes an impact. A single "accessory" needs to have significant scale to please the eye, but you can create the same aesthetic experience through the artful arrangement of multiples. Too much of anything is just annoying, so knowing where to stop is key (designer Nestor Santa-Cruz goes so far as to say that the most glamorous thing you can do in a room is edit). Many of the old rules still apply: Group like objects together; odd numbers are better than even. But rules are made to be broken, especially by the people who made them. Ultimately, art and objects should not just be in a room, but of the room. At best, all the objects relate to the homeowner. Designer Bill Sofield has a Manhattan pied-à-terre that is full of beautifully designed objects, none of them chosen for its style alone: Each has a backstory—which is the way to keep your rooms personal.

■ Nature-loving Seattle architect George Suyama built his modern home overlooking Puget Sound. Every object in the home is as carefully chosen as the building materials. Decorative accessories—from ceramic vases to doll's heads on sculpture stands—are arranged in secular "altars," almost as occasions for meditation.

■ A pair of Key West homeowners created this well-balanced vignette featuring a credenza by Gio Ponti and Franco Albini. An imposing pair of sculptures from the estate of Gianni Versace brackets an impressive collection of art pottery. The three panels of Carl Palazzolo's painting echo the grid on the doors of the midcentury credenza.

■ Don't tell Marjorie Skouras that white is the best background for art. The rule-ignoring Los Angeles designer painted the living room of this Mediterranean manse a vibrant fuchsia and then hung a suite of nine colorful Allen Ruppersberg drawings over the mantel, flanking them with a pair of anonymous Chinese portraits.

■ Todd Oldham's living room in his rural Pennsylvania home is a tribute to artist Charley Harper, whose blithe avian prints dominate. Oldham, who repeated the bird motif in a La-Z-Boy sectional of his own design, even incorporated the room's window grid into his composition; the crowning photograph is by Todd Eberle.

"*Glamorous rooms, just like glamorous people, have something that makes them memorable.*"
—*Benjamin Noriega-Ortiz.*

■ Paola Navone is one of the most accomplished living designers of contemporary Italian furniture (she designed the table pictured here for Gervasoni). In the dining room of her home in Milan, she displays her extraordinary collection of Chinese celadon ceramics on three illuminated, zinc-clad shelves that run the entire length of the room.

*OBJECTS

*Staircases

■ When architect Stuart Silk was hired to renovate this 1901 home on Queen Anne's Hill in Seattle, his mandate was to open the old place up to vistas both exterior and interior. The new view-enhancing glassed-in foyer now features an enormous pivoting door and a steel staircase with no risers and "barely there" treads softened by oak.

The staircase designed by architect William Bennett for this renovated 1857 mill north of Toronto, Ontario, is made of steel set in concrete that was poured into smooth plywood forms. To tie the high-tech stairs to the original building, much of which he preserved, Bennett installed thick treads of reclaimed yellow birch.

Among the visual conventions of the Houston home architect Christopher Robertson designed for his philanthropic parents are the interplay of hard reflective surfaces like mahogany and glass with unexpected softening curves. Back when he was a mere senator, President Obama spoke from the pulpit-like landing of this staircase.

Working with longtime collaborators—metal artisan Dennis Luedeman and structural engineer Paul Endres—San Francisco-area architect Anne Fougeron created a stunning loft-conversion staircase of blackened hot-rolled steel with tapered treads and no risers whatever, then defined its volume with a see-through wire-mesh "wall."

"Staircases should always be grand." —Benjamin Noriega-Ortiz

If your first thought on hearing the word "staircase" is the scene from the musical film *Funny Face* where Audrey Hepburn runs down the steps of the Louvre with the chiffon shawl of her red gown unfurling behind her, recalling the winged Nike of Samothrace on the landing above her, then chances are, your taste runs to glamour. No architectural element of a house is inherently grander than a grand staircase. In any plan for a new home or a serious renovation, the staircase should be considered long and early, because it is large and expensive, and, in the world of glamour, it is much more than a means of accessing the upper floors. Yet it's also more than the set for a dramatic entrance. Staircases are highly desirable among homeowners (hence the popularity of "center stair colonials"). They are also often the first things seen when entering a house. Further, they represent the nature and character of their homes instantly. Because a staircase is a necessary, practical element and a large number of code rules dictate its construction, each one presents a great opportunity to pull out all the creative design stops. Deciding just how those treads and risers should relate to each other—or if there should be visible risers at all—is crucial, whichever style you choose for your home.

Previous spread, left: For a new home in Berkeley that is marked by openness, architect David Wilson designed this sculptural steel-and-walnut staircase to the master bedroom suite. The open-riser design helps give the staircase a sense of floating; its craftsmanship is as meticulous as the antique Korean chest that stands beside it.

Previous spread, right: Darryl Wilson's stunning black-and-white renovation of this 1960s house in the Hollywood Hills features a new staircase that is a single sweep of poured lightweight terrazzo, a seamless application; keeping the ovals of the blued-steel railings upright was one of the engineering challenges of the unique structure.

When designer Kelly Hoppen renovated this converted London loft (which once belonged to the queen's only nephew), she installed a "spiral" staircase that she carpeted in practical sisal in a neutral tone that perfectly fits the home's palette. The staircase leads to a "chill-out" area designed for relaxation and meditation.

The staircase of this Tucson, Arizona, residence—designed for clients who love the outdoors by architect Arthur Andersson—is the spine of the house. The polished-concrete steps sweep up from the open foyer to the bedrooms and down into the library. The natural materials were all chosen to relate the house to the surrounding earth.

"When a staircase is married appropriately to the architecture, it can be beautifully sculptural." —Darryl Carter

"What could be more glamorous than stepping down a sweeping and sensuous staircase?" —Raji Radhakrishnan

*Fireplaces

■ Toronto designer Elaine Cecconi, half of the partnership of Cecconi Simone, separated her dining and living rooms with this black fireplace made of Corian with the monumental simplicity of modern sculpture. Suspending the chimney piece from the ceiling, creates a pass-through between the floor-level gas fire and the fluted hood.

"Fireplaces are always glamorous in a modern setting."
—Larry R. Laslo

Any real estate agent will tell you: Home buyers love fireplaces. Fireplaces are the new spa bathrooms of the real estate world. It's not surprising. Who doesn't look good sitting around in the warm glow of firelight? Ever since our prehistoric ancestors figured out that a hole in the roof was a good way to keep the fire from filling their cave with smoke, fireplaces have played a core part in the design of homes. For centuries, homes affluent enough to have one were built around the fireplace, since it provided warmth for the family as well as a convenient place to braise the evening brisket. There seems to be something universal in the appeal of fire, which, after all, is one of the four basic "elements" (water, air, and earth being the other three). Virtually all new upmarket homes have fireplaces, as do many renovations. One of the great things about them is that, once you've installed the actual mechanism of the firebox, your fireplace surround can be almost anything you want it to be, from adobe to stainless steel, from brick to Corian—and it can change whenever your decorating style evolves. Wherever you install your fireplace—living room, bedroom, kitchen, or bath—the space becomes instantly more inviting because it invites you to spend some quality time.

■ In the master bedroom of a new home in Los Angeles by architect William Hefner and his wife and business partner, interior designer Kozuko Hoshino, a daybed cozies up to an elevated fireplace in a travertine wall with a radically simple mantelpiece; the fireplace also opens into the master bathroom, artfully facing the tub.

■ If the Jetsons opened a ski lodge, this home in Green Bay, Wisconsin, by Chicago architect Douglas Garofalo might be it. Shrewd choices of colors, materials, and furnishings help warm the living room, as does the FireOrb, a podlike sculptural fireplace of Garofalo's design that simply hangs from the ceiling.

■ Contractor Jim Dow's masculine Zen makeover of his Seattle home brought new materials and streamlined detailing to the most standard building components. In the living room, he used blackened steel for the frames of new windows on each side of the soaring fireplace and again on the log boxes he devised for storage.

■ When husband-and-wife architects Cathi and Steven House designed this home in Marin County, California, they created a simple two-sided fireplace between the music and dining rooms. Rigorously modern, it's finished in burnt-orange Venetian plaster, a technique deeply rooted in history (like the antique chair beside it).

■ For a major renovation, designers William Diamond and Anthony Baratta respected the neoclassical conceits of this 1980s Connecticut home, but the bedroom fireplace is pure 21st century, with metal details on a surround made of Neopariés, a crystallized-glass material. The andirons are custom, by Diamond Baratta.

For a house in Dallas created by architect Mark Domiteaux and designer Nancy Leib, a fireplace that stands between the kitchen and the family room is composed of concrete, Venetian plaster, gray limestone tile from Ann Sacks, and stainless steel; the sculpture is by Cayle Cox Metal Fabrication.

The surprising renovation of this typical cottage in Key West, Florida, was designed by architect Rob Delaune, an expert in working with the city's strict historic preservation mandates. The living room features a gas fireplace in a dramatic stainless steel surround that rises to the building's roofline.

"We tend to think that polish is glamorous, but I think matte and rough textures can be glamorous, too. It's all about the mix and balance within a room." —Nestor Santa-Cruz

"Glamour is the effect a room has on the people in it. A room can be completely empty, but if it evokes a particular frame of mind, it can be glamorous." —Kelly Monnahan

*Drapery

In the living room of this elegant, surprisingly spacious 750-square-foot apartment in Milwaukee, designer Joel Agacki left the windows undraped but covered a full interior wall with floor-to-ceiling sheers that soften and add romance to the room. Then he hung art in front of and behind the folds for an air of added mystery.

"No room is glamorous without the use of flowing fabrics."
—Benjamin Noriega-Ortiz

Back in the 1950s, there was an odd vogue for Technicolor films based on the more salacious Bible stories (*Samson and Delilah* or *Salome,* for example). And almost all of these films had at least one scene where diaphanous drapes thirty or forty feet high fluttered in a scented breeze between the pillars of some femme fatale's ill-gotten palace. Those billowing yard goods set the standard for a certain kind of glamorous fantasy. Today drapery is more than a matter of window treatments. In fact, a contemporary room may have nothing at all on the windows, light being held in such high regard by modern homeowners and designers alike. "Artfully nude" is one of the favored window treatments of the earliest 21st century. But drapery is no longer confined to windows. Fabrics of all kinds—from the sheerest silks to the heaviest velvets—hang in doorways between rooms and on interior walls and as lines of demarcation in open spaces. There is a decided trend among designers to combine different fabrics, often of contrasting textures, in single drapery panels and to "cheat" the height of rooms by extending the drapes up to the ceiling. Whatever you use, fabric in a glamorous modern-day setting needs to have a luxurious hand, to hang beautifully, and to pleat deeply.

■ The variations in straight drapery panels are enormous. In this Hollywood-Mediterranean home, designer Mark Cutler canopied the master bed in sheer fabric that reminds the homeowners of their honeymoon in Bali; the windows feature a somewhat more substantial fabric, but it is close in color to the romantic bed curtains.

■ In this Boston loft, designer Frank Roop created visual interest and architectural presence with drapery panels made by stitching horizontal bands of fabrics that contrast in texture, hand, and weight. The double-height living room drapes pair white sheers with a bluish-gray linen that picks up the tones of the adjacent den.

■ For these fashionably puddled drapes in a wood-paneled Atlanta library, designer Jill VanTosh paired two different shimmering bronze fabrics—one sheer, one opaque—alternating them vertically, like stripes, allowing light through the windows while maintaining the elegance of the room. They hang from chunky rings on a room-long rod.

"A window treatment doesn't have to be complicated or tortured to be glamorous."
—Larry R. Laslo

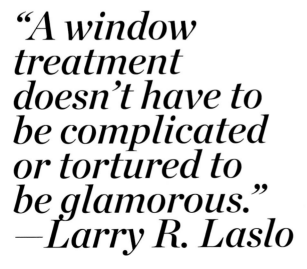

For the main bedroom in a colorful apartment he designed in Manhattan's Chelsea neighborhood, Jamie Drake made a deep horizontal border by turning the bright pink and fuchsia Cowtan & Tout silk at right angles to itself. The border is as deep as the adjacent armchair, giving the border the character of wainscoting.

Up the ante on romance in any room with window treatments that feature volume, movement, and a sensual touch. In this meticulously green Seattle penthouse by SkB Architects, draperies in the master suite are made of alternating vertical panels of mohair and silk in a spectrum of neutrals that recapitulates the light, earthy palette.

Being treated like any other room of the house is part of the glamour of the new bathroom. Designer Betsy Burnham installed floor-to-ceiling taupe gabardine drapes in this Beverly Hills bachelor's home (it features numerous men's suiting fabrics throughout). Raising curtain rods to the ceiling generally makes rooms seem taller.

New York City designer William Sofield's pied-à-terre on a tree-lined Greenwich Village street is on the parlor floor of a historic townhouse. In his living room, Sofield hung extravagant cashmere drapes from gold-toned rods. "Real glamour is rooted in practicality," he says of the curtains, which insulate against chill winter drafts.

■ Previous spread, left: When updating a 1920s Mediterranean villa in Los Angeles, designer Marjorie Skouras kept the elaborate parquet floors in the dining room, but hung simple white shades on the French doors (an echo of Kevin Riley's chandelier). The entrance to the room is marked by heavy silk portieres.

■ Previous spread, right: Greg Agacki used interior draperies to create a soft-edged entrance corridor in this Milwaukee flat. The free-flowing fabric tempers the linearity of the Snaidero kitchen system and keeps the guests from having to enter through the kitchen. Curtain boundaries seem less confining than walls.

■ Faced with a wall of windows over eleven feet high, color-friendly San Francisco–based designer Jay Jeffers devised a curtain that is grand enough for an opera house. At the same time, it is made of a sheer linen that diffuses light but doesn't interrupt the hillside views from the music room, relaxing the separation between inside and out.

■ In the library of this Los Angeles home, designer Mark Cutler covered the windows with Indian saris that he had dyed a deep chocolate color and then made into unique Roman shades. The fabric not only provides a sense of world travel and pleasantly unexpected detail, but the border serves as the room's primary decorative element.

■ Following page: The dining room of this Los Angeles home by architect William Hefner and designer Kazuko Hoshino features floor-to-ceiling curtains made of chain mail from Cascade Coil to separate it from the adjacent hallway. The *Planet* chandeliers are by Umberto Asnago for Georgetti. The white stone on the wall is travertine.

"*To be glamorous, drapes must break or pool. Nothing else works.*" —*John Beckmann*

"*Draperies should not be made of anything you wouldn't want to touch your skin.*" —*Raji Radhakrishnan*

*Chandeliers

■ Modern glamour has a complex but sympathetic relationship to the past. This ornate Italian-glass chandelier reminded Virginia-based designer Barry Dixon of an octopus, which inspired the marine mantel display in a house that he transformed by passing traditional South Florida "Venetian" style through his own sensibility.

■ Architect William Hefner built this home in Los Angeles; the interior designer was Kazuko Hoshino, his wife and business partner. To light the main staircase, they chose a customized version of Bourgeois Bohème's distinctive *Belleville* chandelier. Although they look a bit like ostrich eggs, the elongated globes are handblown glass.

■ For the open staircase of a New Jersey home, a modern update of a classic shingle-style summerhouse, designer Carl D'Aquino and architect Francine Monaco stacked three traditional *Chisolm Hall* lanterns, designed by Michael Amato for the Urban Electric Co., in a decidedly contemporary manner.

■ For the dining room of a New York City apartment—which features mirrored walls, bronze finishes, and brass accents—designer Dan Barsanti chose a 62-inch diameter Jean Karajian chandelier of handblown silvered Venetian glass that's as current as a Dale Chihuly sculpture and reflects light even when it is not the source.

■ Architect Mell Lawrence contrived the one-off "chandelier" over the kitchen area of the great room in this modern Texas ranch house with interior designer Fern Santini, and her husband, contractor Jerre Santini, as an artful mobile of pendant bulbs whose connecting wires are part of the composition.

"I have a chandelier in my kitchen. It definitely ups the glamour quotient." —Jay Jeffers

Call them chandeliers or call them ceiling fixtures (since, technically speaking, a chandelier has branched arms), but whatever you call them, hang one, or more, in any and every room of a glamorous house—and don't be shy about grouping them, either. A light fixture hanging over a table or in a foyer, whether handblown Murano glass or something more minimal, is one of the most common notes in the chamber opera that is glamour. The chandelier, which really is the most practical way of illuminating a dining room, is not generally the best possible way to brighten a room. Architect/designer Hugh Newell Jacobsen dismisses them out of hand as a source of light (and good lighting is now one of the first considerations of good interior designers). Chandeliers are about opulence, elegance, and taking one's place in a long tradition. Today ceiling fixtures come in an enormous range, from the traditional multibranched Venetian glass to modernist flights of fantasy with or without Swarovski crystals. Washington, D.C. designer Darryl Carter likes to modernize traditional chandeliers by stripping off a lot of the crystals. Many new pieces feature frankly geometric arrangements of bulbs, drops, or both. But whatever design appeals to you, let there be ceiling light!

■ Previous spread, left: Hanging chandeliers in unexpected places heighten a sense of glamour. In this Los Angeles home, architect Scott Joyce and designer Susan Young placed a large, rectangular version of Ochre's modern *Light Drizzle* fixture, with its multiple clear-glass drops, alongside the sheer glass portal wall of the main entrance.

■ Previous spread, right: One of the most popular of the pared-down, contemporary (and overscale) chandeliers is this *Tippet* hanging lamp by Kevin Reilly (custom through Holly Hunt). It is shown here in the dining room of Chicago designer Kara Mann, who used it as a pale element in the apartment's high-contrast palette.

■ Chandeliers do not need to be made from obviously glamorous materials to be glamorous themselves. In this rustic-chic Seattle dining room, which features a slab redwood table on piers salvaged from the 1906 San Francisco earthquake, the chandeliers are Portuguese crab pots fitted with simple electric glass lanterns.

■ When designer Shamir Shah was commissioned to freshen a Hamptons house by famed Japanese architect Shigeru Ban, he turned to New York City–based sculptor Susan Etkin for a custom dining room chandelier made of colored and mercury glass (the olive-green globes pick up a similar color in a custom-designed rug).

"Chandeliers are one of my favorite decorative accessories. I love the combination of traditional frames with unexpected dressing—coral, turquoise, feathers." —Marjorie Skouras

■ Among the most successful of contemporary lighting designers is Georgia-born artist David Weeks. Known for combining industrial materials and organic shapes, he fashions mobile-like fixtures (available through Ralph Pucci). He was a perfect fit for the dining area of this San Antonio loft conversion by Jim Poteet and Patrick Ousey.

*Mirrors

In the dining room of this sophisticated high-rise apartment in Chicago by architect Howard Holtzman and designer Douglas Levine, a wall of space-expanding mirror is paneled to echo clear-glass French doors to the living room. Not to miss a reflective moment, the room was fitted with a custom-made mirrored buffet.

■ For a bit of sophisticated reflection in the living room of this Park Avenue duplex apartment, designer Arthur Dunnam of Jed Johnson Associates mirrored the top surface of a custom-made console table. Mirror is durable and easy to clean, but everything used beside it, or on it, must be worthy of visual duplication.

■ This glamorous powder room in a green Seattle penthouse by the creative team at SkB Architects gets its magic from Jo Braun's mosaic inspired by trees. It is made from broken bits of old salvaged mirrors, but any bad luck that might be associated with the project would have to be offset by the aesthetic value of the result.

■ Designer Dan Barsanti mirrored the walls of this Manhattan foyer to expand the space. He also created a bronze-finished grid overlaying the mirror to break up the reflection (the geometry matches the living room doors; the patina is picked up in the console). Barsanti papered the ceiling in an approximation of gold leafing.

■ Working in a tiny New York bedroom, designer Matthew Webb (now co-principal of White Webb in New York City) played with mirrors and shapes by hanging a wall mirror with a square-framed flower in the middle opposite a fish-eye mirror inserted, medallion-like, into the edge of a signature custom-made upholstered headboard.

"The first thing I'd buy for a glamorous room is a mirrored piece of furniture."—Jamie Drake

It is no accident that the grandest of grand salons in that bellwether of glamour, the palace of Versailles, is known as the Hall of Mirrors (although, truth be told, it is somewhat smaller in real life than it has been portrayed in a number of films that have given it the dimensions of a football field). Lit with enfilades of candle chandeliers and torchères encrusted with gilt putti, it must have made a dazzling setting for Marie Antoinette and her full-skirted aristocratic cohorts. Long suspect for its association with the deadly sin of vanity ("Mirror, mirror on the wall"), mirror—glass with a silvered back coating—appeals to interior designers and decorators for the capacity it has for expanding a space, making it nigh on infinite when one mirror is hung opposite another. Today any glamorous room is likely to have at least one special mirror hanging in it (or leaning seductively against an otherwise blank wall). Lately, designers have been going even further, devising applications of mirror that cross the line into architecture, sometimes creating visual ambiguity to enrich the aesthetic experience of a space. Mirrored furniture is especially in vogue, providing instant interest. Mirrors can also make furniture disappear, expanding the sense of space even further.

■ For his Chicago clients' winter home in Miami Beach, the French-born designer Martial (one name only) hung a grid of round convex mirrors on a black living room wall, not only giving the place more visual space, but evoking the portholes of a classic luxury liner and creating an artwork that plays with positive and negative space.

■ To create depth in the entryway of this renovated Coconut Grove, Florida, house, designer Andrew Frank hung a piece of art on a mirrored wall that reflects the hallway it faces (as well as the Alex Katz portrait of Zac Posen that greets arriving visitors), maximizing interest in what would otherwise be a standard plasterboard wall.

■ Almost any room decorated by designer Vicente Wolf will have at least one mirror in it, usually enormous or exotic or otherwise extremely intriguing to look at. In this Long Island home, he installed framed mirror in long horizontal stripes that read almost like wall paneling. These mirrors, he says, create a sense of movement.

■ For a client's new apartment, Washington, D.C.-based designer Darryl Carter, who favors white-on-white rooms and antique accessories, created a pristine, modern powder room and made it doubly glamorous with a mirror in an ornate, 19th-century, gold-toned Italian frame, proving that rigorous editing can be a room's best friend.

■ In the master bedroom of her Miami Beach cottage, retailer Nisi Berryman of NIBA Home went all out, turning extreme femininity modern with a Baroque-inspired mirror the size of a headboard. For more shine, she had the frame silver-leafed. The vintage mirrored vanity is served by an acrylic *Lola* chair of Berryman's design.

"The most glamorous thing about a bathroom is the vanity and how the mirror relates to it." —Kelly Monnahan

"I make a lot of Lucite and mirrored pieces of furniture—they add instant glamour. Colored mirror can be a great modern twist." —Marjorie Skouras

*Daybeds

"Sheen" was one of designer Celerie Kemble's operative words in the design of this 69th-floor apartment overlooking Central Park. In the master bedroom, a deco-inspired sleigh-style J. Alexander chaise in Macassar ebony is upholstered in a champagne velvet that reflects light from the floor-to-ceiling windows.

"Having the time to daydream is the ultimate luxury." —Jamie Drake

History is full of ironies, and one of them is the association of daybeds, a form as old as Western civilization, with an aristocratic lifestyle. Thank painter Jacques-Louis David and his 1800 painting of French beauty Madame Récamier lounging in her form-clinging white neoclassical gown on a piece of furniture that came to take her name. (It's as if the French Revolution and the subsequent Reign of Terror had little effect outside the world of fashion.) Today's daybeds, chaises, lounges, and similar opportunities for decorous reclining appeal to designers for many reasons. One is the visual impact a daybed makes in a room. Often sculptural, they are also highly versatile: Some are designed so that you can sit on them facing forward or back. Whatever you call them, or whichever variation you choose, they have the virtue of forcing a room into a nontraditional deployment of furniture because daybeds, generally speaking, are not designed to be pushed up against the wall. (Designers love pulling furniture off the walls, even in smallish rooms—it is a counterintuitive move that subliminally expands one's perception of space.) A daybed instantly gives a room a jolt not only of casual elegance but of comfort, paramount to good room design, no matter the look or style.

■ When you start with a Golden Age of Hollywood home once owned by silent-screen siren Pola Negri, it is hard not to get carried away and go over the top. Designer Mark Cutler kept the excesses in check in this updated Dream Factory living room, which features a versatile two-way daybed in a crisp, understated fabric.

■ When your bedroom is bigger than many a living room, chances are that you are living the glam life (especially if your bedroom actually has a separate living area in it). Designer David Mitchell created this reading and resting area in a Maryland master suite with a tailored Donghia daybed and slim, contemporary tables and lamps.

■ For the master bedroom of this Adolfo Perez renovation near Boston, designer Susan Orpin contrived to create a gender balance for her married clients by pairing "feminine" fabrics and deep upholstery (like a tufted *Classic* daybed by French artist Patrick Naggar from Ralph Pucci) with a more "masculine" neutral palette.

"Daybeds, recamiers and/or chaises longues are the modern replacement for twin beds in the guest room (please)."
—Darryl Carter

■ Designer Judi Male's clients for this high-rise Miami condo own serious furniture as well as museum-quality art, so placing it all harmoniously took some finessing. To sit beside a Frank Stella painting in the master suite, Male chose a sensuous Vladimir Kagan *Erica* lounge that sits on sheets of intersecting Plexiglas.

■ To furnish this rammed-earth home by Studio B Architects in Aspen, Colorado, designer Larry R. Laslo looked to refined furnishings, including an antique Biedermeier-style burl-wood daybed upholstered in leather. He also selected the 1962 *Arco* lamp by the Castiglioni brothers for Flos, now an icon of modern glamour.

"I love daybeds. They are the perfect perch for one or two, romantic either way. They are used for lounging or entertaining and imply a sense of luxury and timelessness."
—Carl D'Aquino

*ROOMS

■ Creative couple John and Janet Jay of Studio J clearly understand the new mix, the "eclectic current" of interior design. Their Portland, Oregon, living room mixes antique, vintage, and modern furniture. Palette and pattern are limited; the visual focus of the room is on lively art, and material textures range from Plexiglas to woven rattan.

*Living Rooms

LINE VOLUME
LINE IN OUT
AUX TAPE
POWER
PHONO
LED
LINE
MIC
CROSS FADE
LINE VOL
ARM
PITCH
ON OFF
CROSSFADE
AIR RELIVER
BIG AMP
LEVEL
MIXER
TREBLE
BRAIN
"MET"
OHKI

"Glamour, like beauty, is in the eye of the beholder." —Scott Joyce

Today's top designers know that a home should reflect the people who inhabit it, just as their clothes do. There is no one acceptable style except the one that is most personal, most becoming. After all, it doesn't matter how much you love chartreuse: If you don't look good in it, you shouldn't wear it. So, bespoke or prêt-à-porter, rooms should be as personally relevant as attire. The one generalization that is true about living rooms these days is that designers are now asked by clients to restore the "living" to the room, making it pertinent and practical for day-to-day existence for families that include children and pets. As new homes become responsibly smaller, homeowners are beginning to cast a suspicious and judgmental eye on space that is not used routinely. And a formal living room, long reserved strictly for entertaining "important" guests, doesn't seem as wise a use of square footage as it once did, even in homes that can boast separate family rooms. Living rooms are no longer just for company. They do, however, need to accommodate guests, some of whom we may be entertaining for the first time. These most public of rooms, often the largest in the house, present a particularly fertile field for stating the design leitmotifs of the home.

"Every house needs one red room," says Los Angeles designer Marjorie Skouras, "even if it is just the powder room." Her own home in Hollywood features this crimson living room, with its assemblage of periods and styles, from the 18th-century Venetian settee to zebra-print tablecloths and circa 1925 fleece-covered caravan chairs.

■ Architect William Reese created this minimalist Hamptons living room with natural materials and Zen-like proportions. Visual interest comes from variations in texture and light, and decor that pairs cylinders—bark drums, over-scale lamp shades, and silvered ceramic side tables—with Mies chairs and a classic carpet.

■ When New York-based Benjamin Noriega-Ortiz was hired to freshen an Upper East Side apartment that was decorated some 25 years ago by his former boss—the all-star designer John Saladino—he stirred in some of his new favorite things, including an acrylic *Baluster Trestle* table of his own design as a contemporary foil to gilded antiques.

■ To modernize and visually open up the grand salon of this 1912 Paris apartment, American architect Hugh Newell Jacobsen stripped out all the period details except the original oak-parquet floors. In keeping with his preferred neutral palette, he chose clean-lined linen-and-leather *Duc* seating by Mario Bellini for Cassina.

"Marie-Antoinette rode in a carriage, Grace Kelly drove a Porsche, and Angelina Jolie favors her Ducati. All three women offer the ultimate proof that every era is glamorous in its own right." —Kara Mann

■ Designer Andrew Frank helped the owner of this 1963 Coconut Grove home update the hot, tropical, retro glamour of Florida's midcentury heyday. The living room features vintage pieces along with antiques (like a pair of 1782 Louis XVI chairs upholstered in leather in the 1940s); the deco-inspired print fabric is cut velvet.

"The least glamorous thing you can do in a room is over-design it. It looks like you tried too hard or have on too much makeup."
—John Beckmann

"When a client asks for a glamorous room, what they really want is a room that stands out for its sense of style."
—Benjamin Noriega-Ortiz

■ The ebonized-oak floor of this 1980s house in Atlanta (interior design by Jill VanTosh) makes the white palette seem more ethereal. The room, with its new but traditional architectural details, modern furniture, and sheer draperies, is part antebellum South, part 21st-century Milan. The mirror over the added fireplace hides a television.

■ Chicago designer and showroom owner Kara Mann not only went for high contrast in her own apartment living room, but she switched the usual parameters, painting walls and trim the same dark espresso in a glossy finish and choosing furniture (much of it by Christian Liaigre) upholstered in softening fabrics with matte textures.

For the living room of his mid-century Palm Springs house, L.A. designer Michael Berman kept the look "martini cool." His iconic Warren Platner wire chairs are classics of the swinging sixties; the oversized houndstooth fabric on the swivel chair could be right off the runways of London or Paris, back in the day or just last season.

■ Miami design retailer Nisi Berryman, owner of NIBA Home, pulled out all the Caribbean chromatic stops to make a big impression in this relatively small living room. The hot-green walls (Benjamin Moore's *Dark Celery*) and saturated reds give the room the look of a contemporary gift wrapped up in all the right colors.

■ This page: Nothing could be more modern than blurring the lines between the indoors and out. This "living room" is actually a screened porch added to a 1940s home outside Minneapolis by architect Julie Snow and her colleagues. It has its own fireplace, a swinging daybed, and a sculptural *Lovenet* chair by Ross Lovegrove.

■ Previous spread, left page: For her clients' Greenwich Village redbrick townhouse, architect Karen Jacobson amped up period detailing like egg-and-dart molding (she even moved an existing fireplace) but went contemporary with art and furnishings, including a Poul Henningsen *Artichoke* fixture and accents of stainless steel.

■ Previous spread, right page: For the same clients' beach house, Jacobson worked with a similar palette but with pared-down details. The furniture was inspired by the nearby beach, recalling sea-smoothed pebbles and aged driftwood. Here, the simple fireplace features a screen by John-Paul Philippe that's a work of art.

■ Trey Jordan designed this Santa Fe house for himself with vernacular features that he reinvented, from square ceiling beams inspired by hand-hewn log vigas to a corner fireplace that evokes a traditional kiva without its shape. When he sold the home, new owners kept it simple, with Italian furniture as neutral as the architecture.

■ Because dark colors create intimacy, designer Jill VanTosh went nearly black in this Atlanta dining room, using off-white furniture both antique and modern (the lacquered table is by Patrick Jouin for Cassina). The upholstery color comes from a Sandra Berry glass sculpture; the Venini chandelier by Carlo Scarpa is crystal and chrome.

*Dining Rooms

"A truly glamorous room is always of a piece, everything working in concert." —Matthew White

The new dining room is made for use, even if there is enough space in the home for family meals in the kitchen. Still, many homeowners prefer a "formal dining room" for special guests, holidays, or just so that the cooking clutter isn't visible during the meal. Traditional dining rooms have been the easy rooms of a home to design: one table, some matching chairs, a chandelier, and maybe a sideboard. But new designers have looked to the dining room as a place to experiment with these basic necessities, and nowhere, perhaps, is the big mix more varied. Anything can be a table: All you need is a flat surface and a base that doesn't interfere with diners' feet. Anything can be pressed into service—from slabs of timber to salvaged factory doors or slices of piers—and many designers take particular delight in designing custom tables (the better to get exactly the look and size they need). More likely than not, the six or eight or ten chairs do not all match (they may each be unique). Banquettes and benches have become popular as seating on one side of the table. Homeowners have also been opting for multiple tables that fit together to become one long groaning board for the family Thanksgiving but can be taken apart for card parties or more intimate suppers.

■ For a midcentury-inspired apartment overlooking Central Park, designer Amy Lau purchased a room divider consisting of 196 glass tiles, then deconstructed it and turned it into a reflective piece of art for a dining room largely occupied by a contemporary BDDW table and vintage *String* chairs by Jacques Guillon.

■ Manhattan designer Vicente Wolf gave this Long Island dining room its glamour by wrapping a limestone table with a matching slit-leather skirt, alternating two sets of chairs (four low and luxurious, four elegantly tall), and hanging a David Weeks lighting fixture. The palette was inspired by the sea and sky of Burma.

■ Designer John Beckmann likes "a little bling in every room." In this Greenwich Village dining room, he started with serious furniture by Armani/Casa and Versace and witty accents like the Warhol *Uncle Sam* and a faux-antler chair. The bling is a metal-mesh chandelier by Dominique Perrault that drips with crystals—by Swarovski, no less.

■ Washington, D.C.–based designer Nestor Santa-Cruz prefers rooms in black, white, and gold—or combinations of the same, like this dining room in a client's 1911 townhouse. It features a table he designed of copper and walnut and an unexpectedly overscale neo-Baroque bronze chandelier by Hervé Van der Straeten.

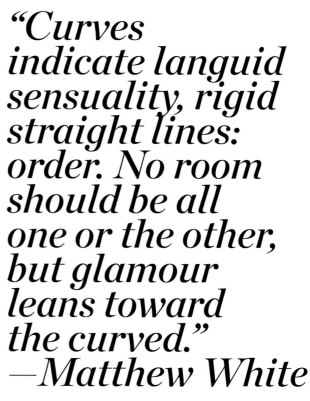

"Curves indicate languid sensuality, rigid straight lines: order. No room should be all one or the other, but glamour leans toward the curved." —Matthew White

■ In a new Atlanta home by architect Keith Summerour, designer Barbara Westbrook created modern glamour with high-sheen Venetian plaster walls. A Lucite pedestal, sisal carpeting, metal chinoiserie armchair, and modern art balance the formal custom table, Donghia chandelier, and silk-damask-upholstered dining chairs.

■ Los Angeles architect Scott Joyce worked with interior designer Susan Young on this Pacific Coast home, where glass dining room walls accordion back to nothing at all. The nail-head trim on the tailored dining chairs echoes the transparent globes of Patricia Urquiola and Elaina Gerotto's *Caboche* chandelier for Foscarini.

■ A northern California empty-nest couple finally decided to do it their way: all white. Maple floors provide the only color in this minimalist Marin County dining room. Verner Panton's molded chairs from Vitra pull up to a custom lazy-Susan table by designer Daren Joy, who also did the home's room-wide walls of built-in storage.

■ Architect William Reese designed this beautifully proportioned Hamptons home so that only four materials meet the eye: concrete, glass, steel, and—as beautifully shown in the dining room—mahogany. The house revels in openness as well as the subtleties of the natural surfaces.

■ Inspired by traditional Asian concepts of scale, symmetry, and repetition, superstar British designer Kelly Hoppen kept the palette simple in this London project for a bachelor client, choosing a chrome-and-lacquer table and Philippe Starck's equally reflective *Louis Ghost* chairs.

■ In the dining room of her own family's New Orleans home, designer Jill Dupré invited Eero Saarinen's 1956 *Tulip* chairs to the table (a neoclassical family piece that belonged to her mother). The home is a montage of old and new, Asian and Occidental; Dupré herself designed the huge contemporary dining room chandelier.

■ Designer Ronald Bricke created this festival of desert-hot spice tones for an all-beige Tucson home by invoking the traditions of Morocco. He covered beige floor tiles with paprika-toned cement, painted the walls *Mango Punch* from Benjamin Moore, adapted old chairs, and hung an antique light fixture from ABC Carpet & Home.

■ The second-floor railing creates a gallery in this renovated Cape Cod in Santa Monica and makes the dining room appear to occupy the foyer. Designer Susan Moses filled the house with furniture that plays against the traditional architecture, including a nostalgic, Sputnik-inspired chandelier.

■ The back of this renovated Atlanta home by San Francisco–based architect Russell E. Sherman provides easy access to the Chattahoochee River. To maximize social flexibility, the owners opted for three Niels Bendtsen X-legged dining tables, three Philippe Starck chandeliers, and an armada of Emeco's aluminum *Navy* chairs.

For this eco-savvy loft conversion in San Francisco's SOMA district, architect Anne Fougeron added refinement with materials like Carrara marble. She established the dining area with a Kyle Bunting rug. Transparent mesh *Meridiana* chairs by Christophe Pillet sit at the head and foot of an *El Dom* table by Hannes Wettstein.

■ Because red stimulates appetite, it is a popular color for dining rooms. In this Manhattan apartment renovation, designer Mihai Radu specified a red wall treatment with orange complements: The chandelier, by Johanna Grawunder, contains three shades of amber glass, which are repeated in the variously hued B&B Italia chairs.

■ The raised dining room of the Houston home built by architect Christopher Robertson features a mahogany floor, soaring ceilings, and a wall made of castle-sized granite blocks. Robertson designed the table and wall-mounted credenza. The *Duna* chairs from Arper are surprisingly upholstered in a supersized pop-art floral fabric.

"*The key to glamour is not caring what anybody thinks of you.*" —Jonathan Adler

"*When I think of glamour I think of 'casual elegance,' a natural ease and simplicity, of having great style and making it seem effortless.*" —Carl D'Aquino

■ Nothing says glamour better than custom installations. At the request of his New York City client (who collects Asian art but does not entertain much), designer Shamir Shah located the dining room in the foyer and created a unique ceiling of 31 rice-paper lanterns that glow above contemporary furniture and a cowhide rug.

■ For his clients' townhouse dining room in Miami Beach, French-born, Chicago-based designer Martial indulged his love of opposites, with black walls and white marble floors. He designed the round table with a Lucite base and concrete top and added reproduction Louis XVI chairs, each upholstered in a subtly different tone of one color.

■ One major piece of furniture can make a room, especially when it has the presence of this gold-leafed stunner by the late Tony Duquette. Designer Mark Schomisch chose it for his own Hollywood home, then designed the chairs as well as lighting fixture (made from Angelo Mangiorotti tube lights from Blackman Cruz).

■ Architect Richard Williams was commissioned to combine three units in this Washington, D.C., high-rise into a single coherent family home. For the dining room, he contrived woven-fiber sliding window panels and glass sliders to close off the adjacent living room. The *Zettel'z 6* chandelier is by German design wit Ingo Maurer.

■ Because he wanted to emphasize the connection between
the inside of this Berkeley home
and nature, architect David Wilson
worked with natural materials
(concrete, stainless steel, and
wood). Elements of the kitchen,
with its California walnut cabinetry,
fit together like the pieces of a
Russian Constructivist sculpture.

*Kitchens

"My favorite glamorous fabrics are stainless steel and leather." —Hugh Newell Jacobsen

There does not seem to be any end in sight to the conversion of the cooking room back to the all-purpose gathering room. Early American homes had only two rooms, a private bedroom and the public kitchen/ dining room where pretty much everything happened. Today's kitchens have an advantage in the glamour sweepstakes because they tend to be made of materials that have an inherent allure: gleaming metals, refined stone (from marble to granite), and, sometimes, exotic woods. Adding to the glamorization of the kitchen is an infusion of light, a proliferation of windows that allow the cook to get a glimpse of life beyond the stove and oven. This transparency is not just about massive amounts of glass (including backsplashes, either in sheets or tiles) but also about opening up the space, both to adjacent rooms and within its own borders. Upper cabinets in particular are being judged as too visually encroaching. They're being eliminated altogether or hung as individual units rather than as batteries of storage, and their doors are more and more often filled with glass of varying kinds. Even the humble "breakfast nook" is being rethought as a home-themed art installation: not just for cornflakes but for conversation and sating aesthetic appetites.

■ Light and dark meet in the kitchen/family room of a Miami home by architect Jorge L. Hernandez. Designers Nikki Baron and Wendy St. Laurent went for a balance between formal and casual elegance with a custom Christian Liaigre *Courier* table, antique glass-fronted storage, and Klismos-inspired chairs from Donghia.

■ The dramatic and highly efficient kitchen in this loftlike Appleton, Wisconsin, house—designed by Phoenix-based architect Wendell Burnette—features an 18-foot-long island topped by stainless steel. The same wood (rotary cut to emphasize the grain) panels a wall of storage that hides all the appliances, including the refrigerator.

"The most glamorous things about kitchens are expansive counters, beautiful lighting, and commercial appliances. The design should accommodate cooking, of course, but all the other activities with equal aplomb."
—*Kelly Monnahan*

■ Vicente Wolf's design for this Hamptons kitchen includes white walls and dark-stained terra-cotta floor tiles. The chunky legs of the marble-topped, stainless-based prep island contrast with spaghetti-thin Italian stools. For maximum transparency, a room-dividing storage wall has glass-fronted doors on both sides.

■ For her own London loft, designer Kelly Hoppen, who pairs white with near black for contrast, played with reflective and matte surfaces in a charcoal-and-white palette. In the kitchen, stainless steel appliances are set in a wall of wenge wood. The clear hanging *Bubble* chair was originally designed by Eero Aarnio in 1968.

For maximum gleam in this open-end Manhattan kitchen, designer Shamir Shah specified auto-body lacquer for the upper cabinet doors and installed glass tiles as a backsplash and polished St. Laurent marble for countertops. By contrast, the *Orbita* pendant lamps by designer Tomoko Mizu are made of natural bamboo.

■ For their historic Boston home, architects Scott Slarsky and Katarina Edlund created a matched set of marble-topped islands separated by a table. They restored a pair of built-in Federal-style secretaries and a fireplace but added such modern pieces as a Poul Henningsen *Artichoke* chandelier and Philippe Starck *Ghost* chairs.

■ In the capacious kitchen of their home in Portland, Oregon, husband-and-wife designers John and Janet Jay combined Gilbert Rohde chairs from the 1930s with the traditional Japanese lines of a table with a fire-salvaged door as the top. They gave the corner a twist by accessorizing it with a vintage child's pedal car—a Maserati.

■ This fully professional stainless steel and white-oak kitchen designed by architect Frank Welch for Dallas clients is as bright as two skylights, a row of clerestory windows, and multiple glass doors can make it. To warm up the Bulthaup stainless steel, Welch looked to Alvar Aalto for inspiration and installed slats of oak on the ceiling.

"The stove is the heart of the kitchen. It evokes the sense of smell and allows the kitchen to become alive through the art of cooking."
—Carl D'Aquino

■ The breakfast nook in this Atlanta cottage renovated by designer Wendy Blount is a bright window bay that opens onto an adjacent deck. Blount paired Warren Platner wire chairs popular with aficionados of the mid-20th century with traditional wing chairs in a contemporary upholstery pattern from F. Schumacher.

■ The corner eating area of this Park Avenue apartment by Maya Lin (famed for her Vietnam Veterans Memorial in Washington, D.C.) follows the material lead of the kitchen, which features subtly grained wood veneers and concrete floors. Designer Alan Tanksley added the *Luca Meda* chairs to the tufted-leather banquette.

■ There is probably no more popular piece of midcentury furniture than Eero Saarien's table, introduced by Knoll in 1956. For the breakfast area of this Manhattan pied-à-terre, designer Dan Barsanti of Healing Barsanti in Westport, Connecticut, paired a sleek black dining-height table with a custom saddle-stitched leather banquette.

■ The owner of this South Florida home is a passionate collector of 20th-century furniture. Designer Andrew Frank, who helped tame the collection for daily use, created a breakfast area with a rare wood-topped version of the Saarinen table and Mies van der Rohe *Brno* chairs (with flat-steel chrome-plated frames) dated 1929.

■ For a beach house on the New Jersey shore, designer Carl D'Aquino updated traditional blue and white with low-maintenance outdoor fabric by Osborne & Little. Two chairs are by Norman Cherner, the chandelier by Philippe Starck. The high-gloss blue subway tile behind the banquette is an extension of the kitchen's backsplash.

■ This low-slung bay-windowed nook, perfect for lingering breakfasts or late-night snacks, was created by Boston-based architect Kelly Monnahan for a home in Napa, California. Monnahan put a custom marble top on a modified Eames café table base from Herman Miller, surrounding it with swiveling chairs from B&B Italia.

This page: Even industrial loft conversions can be outfitted with glamour, as in this open stainless steel, stained-oak, and polished-concrete kitchen in an 1898 Pittsburgh water-heater factory converted by Dutch MacDonald of Edge Studio. The two-story home features automatic garage doors for quick and easy outside access.

Previous spread, left: When architect Stuart Silk was hired to renovate this Seattle home, he doubled the size of the kitchen and opened it up, but he kept the galley-style room gleamingly simple with pale oak floors, lacquered cabinets, and CaesarStone countertops. The backsplash is a single sheet of back-painted glass.

Previous spread, right: Kitchen designer Matthew Quinn's material choices for this Atlanta project are both deluxe and unexpected, including custom alder-wood cabinetry and a quartz sink from Walker Zanger. He continued the brick backsplash up to the ceiling and created a Euro-chic wall of illuminated glass-fronted storage.

*Bedrooms

■ Washington, D.C.-based designer Nestor Santa-Cruz created the quiet glamour of this Georgetown bedroom with deep, rich fabrics and meticulous detailing. The customized Barbara Barry bed (for Baker) is upholstered in a Rogers & Goffigon cotton/linen blend. The wool-and-cashmere blanket is from Hermès.

"When I think of glamour, I immediately think of a lady's blushy-pink dressing room or boudoir." —Andrew Flesher

As things get more and more chaotic and challenging in the world, bedrooms are becoming more cosseting—and larger—with an emphasis on comfort. Beds are big, often posted and/or canopied, with and without bed curtains. Further, square footage is being reserved for sitting areas that encourage the use of the room not just as a place to sleep but as a sanctum in which to unwind and relax and luxuriate in peace. Bedrooms require places to sleep, of course, but they also need storage, and today's top designers are becoming quite adept at loading bedroom spaces, especially master suites, with built-in, hidden, bonus, and custom-made closets and shelves. Many master suites have desks, of course, but the designs discourage using them for actual work. If one room of the house is to survive as a place not to multitask, it's the bedroom, which is being more frequently designed with an integrated, rather than altogether separate, bathroom. The bedroom, designers and homeowners seem to be saying in unison, should have one purpose: relaxation and rejuvenation. Many clients tell their designers they want their bedrooms to resemble a hotel suite, but a bedroom should never be impersonal. It should be the most personal room in the house.

The less there is in a room, the more perfect each thing has to be. Chicago designer Kara Mann obviously learned this lesson before outfitting her sybaritic monk's cell of a bedroom. Christian Liaigre's one-off canopy bed (draped in sheer *Ballerina* cotton from Great Plains) never went into production.

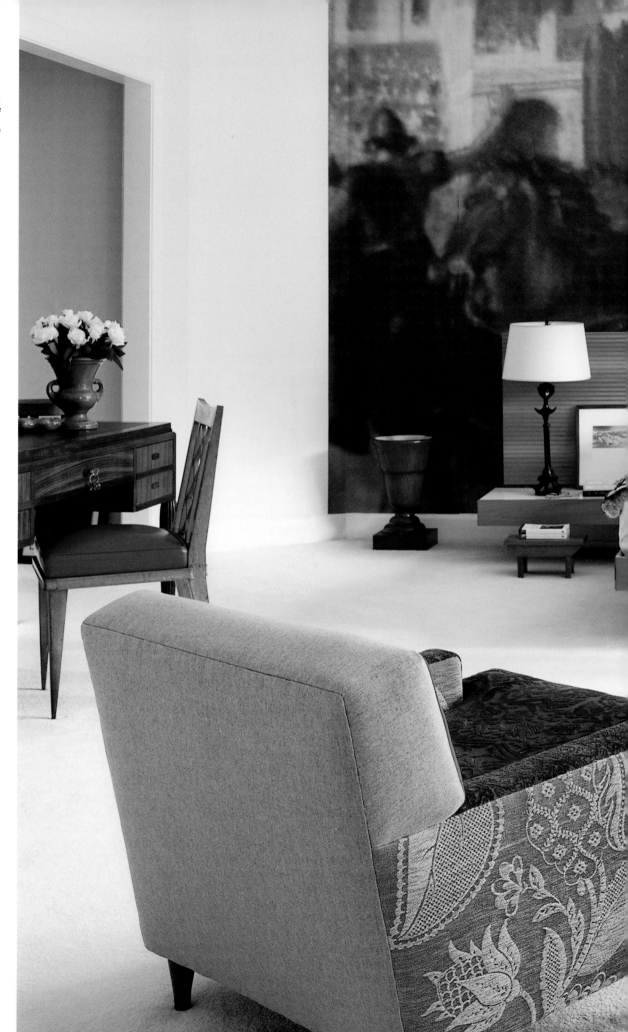

Washington, D.C.-area designer Raji Radhakrishnan likes enormous scale, eccentric mixes, and challenging the orthodoxies of upholstery. In the master bedroom of her suburban Virginia home, she placed a supersized photograph (a fragment of a mural at Versailles) behind the contemporary Design Centro Italia platform bed.

■ Designer Benjamin Noriega-Ortiz believes that monochromatic schemes expand the sense of space, as in this restful lavender room in the northern suburbs of New York City. For softness, he devised a padded headboard with a "slipcover" of Waverly's lilac *Glosheen* that he extended like wainscoting. The Japanese chest and silver mirror are antiques.

■ Every bedroom needs some curves, which Boston architects David Stern and Diane McCafferty provided in their own bedroom with an Antonio Citterio *Apta* chair from Maxalto. In a white room, the designers caution, "form is extremely important: The shape and scale of objects are emphasized in a white environment."

■ "Drywall is never going to add depth to a room," says designer Celerie Kemble. In this New York apartment for a bachelor client, she battened the wall behind the bed in a chocolate suiting fabric and added luster in details, like a pair of unique pendant lamps she had fabricated after her client described them—from a dream.

"The most glamorous thing you can do in a room is wake up surrounded by soft, fresh white linen sheets while bathing in sunlight glistening through sheer white gauzy window treatments."
—Kara Mann

In their Palm Beach apartment, design forces Jonathan Adler and Simon Doonan go traditional, with a four-poster bed, but it's a wowfully mirrored 1970s tour de force by Paul Evans. Keeping true to the precepts of eccentric glamour, the bedcover is a handmade *suzani* from Uzbekistan. Most of the room's accessories are by Adler.

Barry Dixon's Florida clients wanted a romantic bedroom, so he went with a "pale blue and cassis" palette and designed a bed he describes as a "tented folly." The headboard is made from an embroidered Bedouin fabric that had been sewn into pantaloons for a Tunisian wedding garment; bedside table lamps are alabaster.

In New Orleans, designer Brian Bockman went 1950s retro Baroque with tufted, buttoned, piped, and flanged silk douppioni, matching the fabric sheen for sheen with a mirrored side table, polished ebonized walnut floors, and a bedside lamp with small crystal beads, a nod to the headboard buttons.

"Glamorous doesn't have to break the bank, but it should break the mold."
—Vicente Wolf

"A simply furnished monk's cell can be glamorous. Think of the beauty of the natural light coming in from small windows or candlelight at night: White walls, stone floors, and wicker baskets. How chic!"—Nestor Santa-Cruz

■ The serene master bedroom of this Park Avenue duplex, created by Arthur Dunnam of Jed Johnson Associates, features calming symmetry, a light decorative hand, and furniture of his own design. Both the bed and the nightstands are made of ebonized mahogany and bleached wenge, a wood that is more popular in darker stains.

■ In their Portland, Oregon, home, architects Claudine and Giorgio Lostao of Ridiculous Design struck a uniquely satisfying balance of wit and refinement. Claudine made the "tapestry" and Giorgio painted it, complete with nonworking fireplace. An antique dentist's cabinet stands beside a sleek *Tokyo* bed designed by Piero Lissoni for Porro.

■ In this Washington, D.C., bedroom, designer Darryl Carter pulled out his signature stops: a creamy beige-on-white palette with dark accents in natural wood. He played the refinement of the platform bed, Klismos chair, and 19th-century burl-oak screen against the rough-hewn texture of the reclaimed barn-wood floor.

■ This study in ivory (with ebony floors) is in a 1980s Atlanta house made grand by designer Jill VanTosh with modern furniture and old-world inspiration, including an enthusiastic *Fenice* chandelier by Gian Paolo Canova for Axo and theatrical draperies. It all comes together in a room that could be the set of a Mozart comic opera.

"A room must have wit to be glamorous. Any design that seems over-considered or over-serious ain't glamorous."
—Jonathan Adler

Kara Mann expanded and designed this Victorian house in Chicago for clients with two young sons. The master bedroom is a relaxing retreat where indoor and outdoor nature meet, from faux wood wallpaper to an antique wool carpet from Morocco. Lacy drapes with a slight break in them complement the substantive furniture.

■ The Aspen, Colorado, home that Washington, D.C.–area architect Hugh Newell Jacobsen designed for clients maximizes indoor glamour with spectacular views. In the bathroom, an aptly named *Zen* spout from Lefroy Brooks fills the *Spoon* tub (by Gianpolo Benedini for Agape), which sits like sculpture beside a tall vertical window.

*Bathrooms

"The most glamorous thing about a bathroom is a really big, fabulous bathtub." —Marjorie Skouras

No room of the house has made a more dramatic transformation over the last century than the bathroom. Call it the home's biggest splash. From a closet retrofitted with a commode, the *salle de bain* has become a spacious, spa-inspired playground for adults. Without a doubt, bathroom fixtures—from tubs that look like bathing vessels for Cleopatra to vessel sinks that are carved, cast, and molded into shapes never before seen outside MoMA—have practically become pieces of design art (and at the prices they fetch, they should only be as good an investment). Although no room has a more practical rationale, none offers such endless possibilities for sybaritic invention. The bathroom is nearly a blank slate. Now the size of the average postwar living room or larger, today's wish-fulfilling bathroom would doubtless stun the Levitts of the world, whose mass-produced homes had six-by-eight-foot family bathrooms, about the size of a latter-day toilet enclosure. Bathrooms incorporate walk-in closets and dressing rooms and boast all the accoutrements of a hair salon or country-club locker room—plus faucets that gleam like tiaras. The newly glamourous bathroom may retain ease of maintenance, but it does not limit the design imagination.

For a renovated Long Island beach house, architect James Merrell and designer Tori Golub created a masterful bathroom around Kohler's infinity-edge *Sok* tub, set in a plaster surround that matches the concrete floor. Furniture includes a Biedermeier settee and a Japanese chest that supports an antique child's hoop.

221

D.C. designer Darryl Carter treats bathrooms like any other room in a house, which in his case means antique or vintage furniture (here, a 1940s French wing chair upholstered in crisp white fabric), as well as big tubs and showers. He used Carrara marble both in slab form and as tile (in the L-shaped, glass-enclosed shower).

In her white-with-black bathroom in London, Kelly Hoppen set sculptural bathtub hardware of her own design into a black box beside the elliptical marble tub by Andrée Putman, which the designer set on a raised, stained-oak platform. The striated marble wall is subtly gridded; the stools are by India Madhavi and Mies van der Rohe.

The master bathroom of this Minnesota renovation by Julie Snow Architects of Minneapolis focuses on an imposing *Cube* tub from WetStyle. The square mirror over the lacquered vanity reflects a wall of one-inch glass tiles from Bisazza (after a design inspired by Moooi, the Dutch design source founded by Marcel Wanders).

"It doesn't get more glamorous than having a lounge chair or chaise in the bathroom."
—Andrew Flesher

■ Just because a powder room is small doesn't mean it can't be glamorous. In this District of Columbia home, designer Lori Graham went all out with a vintage-style marble-topped Waterworks sink, Cole & Son's *Malabar* wallpaper from Lee Jofa, and a pair of crystal-drop sconces from a Georgetown flea market.

■ For a Park Avenue powder room, Matthew Berman and Andrew Kotchen of Workshop/APD layered the walls and ceiling with leather tile. The right-hand wall is an enlarged aerial photograph mounted between sheets of glass and illuminated from behind like a giant decorative light box.

■ This New York City powder room—part of an apartment renovation by architect West Chin—has river-stone floors and zebrawood walls for an Asian flavor. To double the size of the room visually, the designers covered one entire wall with mirror. The wall-mounted, bowed-trough sink is from Boffi.

■ In this Aspen, Colorado, powder room, interior designer Larry R. Laslo (of Manhattan) combined the reflective with the matte: a mirrored wall with a concrete sink and a mahogany vanity shelf. He mounted a contemporary plain mirror a few inches off a wall of mirrored mosaic tile and lit the room with a vintage chandelier.

■ House + House Architects of San Francisco created this powder room in northern California, which features a "floating" walnut shelf for a Vitraform sink. Designer Jay Jeffers thought it would be fun to play up the room's 11-foot height by installing *The Woods* wallpaper from Cole & Son's, with its exaggerated vertical tree print.

■ This SoHo condominium powder room by Shamir Shah pairs dark-glass mosaic tile with a charming bird-friendly, hand-screened wallpaper from Cavern Home. The mirror, with its leather strap and oversize "hook," is from BDDW. Shah assembled the sink from a resin surface, glass legs, and nickel fittings from Urban Archaeology.

A small room can be glamorous— if it twinkles."
—*Jonathan Adler*

■ For the renovation of the 1963 Palm Springs house that Donald Wexler built for singer Dinah Shore, the design team blasted out the back of the building for a phenomenal new bathroom with translucent glass wall tiles and Metalismo floor files (both from Walker Zanger); the two sinks, like simple glass boxes, are from Axolo.

■ The master bathroom that designer John Beckmann created for his Greenwich Village client was inspired by one at the Hotel de Russie in Rome (the homeowner's favorite place to unwind). Urban Archaeology custom-made the gold wall tiles from a photograph, but the tub and tub filler (by Boffi) are Beckmann introductions.

■ For a master bathroom that feels like a vacation, Seattle contractor Jim Dow installed a custom-made, concrete Japanese soaking tub at floor level. The enormous window next to the tub opens onto a matching pool in a privacy garden that makes bathing seem like an outdoor activity. A glass wall separates the adjacent shower stall.

"The most glamorous thing about a bathroom is the shape of the faucets and plumbing fixtures."
—Nestor Santa-Cruz

■ Previous spread, left: Architect Stewart Silk kept the multiple whites of the master bathroom of this Seattle home interesting with variations in the reflective finishes, from the quietly gleaming Ann Saks marble mosaic tiles on the floor to the enamel-like *.25* tub from Waterworks. The *Moheli* chair is by Paola Navone for Orizzonti.

■ Previous spread, right: The expansive master bathing and dressing suite in this Virginia home, designed by architect Mark McInturff, explores new ways of using glass. Here, twin sinks are set in a vanity with a glass top and sides inside a larger glass box frosted on the lower half; behind the sinks is a glass-enclosed tub.

■ This bathroom—in architect Lavinia Fici Pasquina's renovated home in Bethesda, Maryland— seems immediately Asian in inspiration thanks to a shoji-like application of insulated Kalwall and details like the river stone alongside the tub surround. The *Origami* tub is by BainUltra, the *Frozen* sink from Simas.

■ In New Orleans, designer Jill Dupré included a number of Asian decorative accents in her master bathroom, including an occasional pillow of her own design. The vanity, with its twin Kohler sinks, is custom made. The pair of sconces was made by designer Paul Gruer and wired through the mirror.

■ Nothing says Zen relaxation like a Japanese soaking tub. In his own Puget Sound home in Washignton, architect George Suyama—a master at creating a sense of sublime balance—sunk his tub below ground. Beside it, a sliding glass door opens to the outside, where a decorative pool rises to the same height as the bathwater.

"Glamour means transcending time. It connotes beautiful and luxurious spaces that stimulate and calm the senses at the same time."
—Michael Berman

■ This 1960s house on Hollywood Boulevard steps down a steep hillside, giving it panoramic views of L.A. from every floor. When designer Darryl Wilson renovated it, he created this sybaritic bathroom. The floor, bathtub, and countertops with their integral twin sinks are all poured terrazzo; the richly grained wood is ebony.

*Resources

■ Abode, Fern Santini
4414 Burnet Rd., Austin, TX 78756
512-300-2303
www.fernsantini.com

■ Abramson Teiger Architects
8924 Lindblade St., Culver City, CA 90232
310-838-8998
www.abramsonteiger.com

■ Adolfo Perez Architect
69 Union St., Newton, MA 02459
617-527-7442
www.adolfoperez.com

■ Alan Koppel Gallery
210 W. Chicago Ave., Chicago, IL 60610
312-640-0730
www.alankoppel.com

■ Allied Works Architecture, Brad Cloepfil
1532 S.W. Morrison St., Portland, OR 97205
503-227-1737
www.alliedworks.com

■ Allied Works Architecture
12 W. 27th St., 18th Floor, New York, NY 10001
212-431-9476
www.alliedworks.com

■ Amy Lau Design
601 W. 26th St., Suite M272, New York, NY 10001
212-645-6168
www.amylaudesign.com

■ Andersson-Wise Architects,
Arthur W. Andersson
98 San Jacinto Blvd., Suite 2010, Austin, TX 78701
512-476-5780
www.anderssonwise.com

■ Andrew Frank Interior Design
1000 Venetian Way, Miami Beach, FL 33139
212-752-6656

■ Andrew Hollingsworth
www.andrewhollingsworth.com

■ April Sheldon Design
415-541-7773
www.aprilsheldondesign.com

■ Axis Mundi, John Beckmann
315 W. 39th St., Suite 805, New York, NY 10018
212-643-2608
www.axismundi.com

■ Barry Dixon Inc.
8394 Elway Lane, Warrenton, VA 20186
540-341-8501
www.barrydixon.com

■ Blackman Cruz
836 N. Highland, Los Angeles, CA 90038
323-466-8600

■ Blackman Cruz
2021 17th St., San Francisco, CA 94103
415-934-9228
www.blackmancruz.com

■ Blount Design, Wendy Blount
216 14th St. N.W., Atlanta, GA 30318
404-888-0826
www.blountdesign.com

■ Bluegreen Consulting, Monica Smith
98 Union St., Suite 509, Seattle, WA 98101
206-550-9725
www.bluegreendev.com

■ BNO Design,
Benjamin Noriega-Ortiz with Paul Latham
75 Spring St., 6th Floor, New York, NY 10012
212-343-9709
www.bnodesign.com

■ Bockman Forbes + Glasgow, Brian Bockman
2627 DeSoto St., New Orleans, LA 70119
504-942-0200
www.studiobfg.com

■ Bohl Architects
161 Prince George St., Annapolis, MD 21401
410-263-2200
www.bohlarchitects.com

■ Bonura Building
3235 San Fernando Rd., Building No. 5,
Los Angeles, CA 90065
323-478-0101
bonurabuilding.com

■ Burnham Design
523 S. Rimpau Blvd., Los Angeles, CA 90020
323-857-1854
www.burnhamdesign.com

■ Cecconi Simone, Elaine Cecconi
1335 Dundas St. West,
Toronto, Ontario, Canada M6J 1Y3
416-588-5900
www.cecconisimone.com

■ John Chrestia,
Chrestia Staub Pierce Interiors & Architecture
7219 Perrier St., New Orleans, LA 70118
504-866-6677
www.cspdesign.com

■ Christopher Coleman Interior Design
55 Washington St., Suite 707, Brooklyn, NY 11201
718-222-8984
www.ccinteriordesign.com

■ Courtney & Company
9412 Gaylord, Houston, TX 77024
713-665-5600
www.courtneyandcompany.com

■ D. Crosby Ross
9200 W. Sunset Blvd., # 635,
West Hollywood, CA 90069
310-859-7320

■ D'AquinoMonaco
214 W. 29th St., Suite 1202, New York, NY 10001
212-929-9787
www.daquinomonaco.com

■ Darryl Carter Inc.
2342 Massachusetts Ave. N.W.,
Washington, D.C. 20008
202-234-5926
www.darrylcarter.com

■ Darryl Wilson
8440 Santa Monica Blvd., Suite 201,
West Hollywood, CA 90069
www.darrylwilsondesign.com

■ David Hotson Architect,
David Hotson & Steve Angelo
176 Grand St., 2nd Floor, New York, NY 10013
212-965-8828
www.hotson.net

■ David Jameson Architect
13 South Patrick St., Alexandria, VA 22314
703-739-3840
www.davidjamesonarchitect.com

■ Deborah Berke and Partners Architects
220 Fifth Ave., New York, NY 10001
212-229-9211
www.dberke.com

■ Design Galleria, Matthew Quinn
351 Peachtree Hills Ave., N.E., Suite 234,
Atlanta, GA 30305
404-261-0111
www.designgalleria.net

■ Design Resource Center, Lisa Zack
890 Elm Grove Rd., Elm Grove, WI 53122
262-797-7883
www.drcdesign.com

■ designLAb Architects, Scott Slarsky
711 Atlantic Ave., Boston, MA 02111
617-350-3005
www.designlabarch.com

■ Diamond Barratta Design
270 Lafayette St., New York, NY 10012
212-966-8892
www.diamondbarattadesign.com

■ DiCicco Vinci Architects
135 Fifth Ave., New York, NY 10010
212-676-5495
www.dva-vinci.com

■ Domiteaux Architects
4603 W. Lovers Ln., Dallas, TX 75209
214-691-8388
www.domiteaux.com

■ Drake Design Associates, Jamie Drake
315 E. 62nd St., 5th Floor, New York, NY 10021
212-754-3099
www.drakedesignassociates.com

■ E. Cobb Architects Inc., Eric Cobb
911 Western Ave., Suite 318, Seattle, WA 98104
www.cobbarch.com

■ Edge Studio, Dutch MacDonald
5411 Penn Ave., Pittsburgh, PA 15206
412-345-5005
www.edge-studio.com

■ Edlund + Haas Design
531 Massachusetts Ave., #1, Boston, MA 02118
617-899-8023
edlundhaasdesign.com

■ Eric Ceputis Design
701 Ingleside Place, Evanston, IL 60201
847-864-1124

■ FAB Architecture, Patrick Ousey
402 Josephine St., Austin, TX 78704
512-469-0775
www.fabarchitecture.com

■ Form Architecture + Interiors
88 E. 10th St., New York, NY 10003
212-206-6430
www.formarch.com

■ Frank Roop Design + Interiors
224 Clarendon St., Suite 31, Boston, MA 02116
617- 267-0818
www.frankroop.com